Poems from Down Under

JOHN ROSS

Illustrated by Darya Kazakova

Our Big Land

What is there outside your window? Rain, sun or cloudy gloom?
Jungle, forest, sandy beach, bush or scrub or dune?
In Australia we've got the lot, depends how much it rains.
In the north it just can't stop, down south its sunlit plains.

The mighty central desert just sits quietly and bakes,
All rocks and sand, insects and birds, small animals and snakes.
Go further west, it's slowly back to rainfall, sheep and wheat.
There's gumtree shade in the paddocks, and grass for stock to eat.

In the south the gentle rains have sheep and cattle grazing,
And so, wherever you might go, our land is quite amazing.

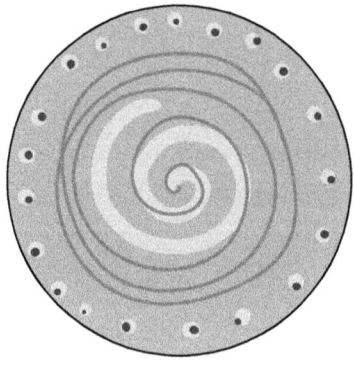

Our First People

Been here 40,000 years, the first people of this land
They had a way of living only they can understand
They foraged, fished and hunted, they travelled far and wide
And they took their spirits with them, the truths they knew inside

Our lonely land was full to them with dreaming tales alive
Told down through the ages and passed on from tribe to tribe.
The coming of the colonists disrupted the long story
They first brought convicts, not marauders seeking wealth and glory.

Yet they heedlessly drove the old ones out, tramped on their dreaming places,
But now we all must try to find a reckoning of the races.
Voices, treaties, plans and schemes seem to vanish in hot air.
The road to good intentions isn't leading anywhere.

Respect and welcome, yes, but talk is the stuff of fools.
We need houses, jobs and welfare, hospitals and schools.
We need a living for our people, it's time to lift the trap.
We all need to stand and say, 'For God's sake, Close the Gap.'

A Nature Wonderland

Way back in the darkest ages, our mighty planet rumbled.
It's insides sort of bubbled up, the land above got jumbled.
The bottom pieces fell away, the sea filled up the zone,
Our birds and animals and trees were stranded, all alone,
Thriving and surviving in the land in rain and shine.
They had been here for ages, so they got along just fine.

They could not leave, but other creatures couldn't reach our ground,
That's why the kangaroo and other Aussie favourites abound.
Koalas, quokkas, numbats, wombats roam around at will,
While kookaburras, lyrebirds and parrots squawk and trill.

The first explorers reeled in shock at the sight of the black swan,
They only knew of white ones in the land that they came from.
Tasmania also split away, became a separate land,
Letting Tassie Tigers, Tassie Devils prosper and expand.

The new settlers brought in cattle, sheep and pigs and goats to farm.
They helped to make us rich but they did our nature harm.
Unluckily some also brought in blackberries, foxes, rabbits,
Which spread out very quickly, they had spreading sort of habits.

They attacked our wildlife as they rampaged across the land,
Sweeping through our bushland, jungles, even desert sand.
So, our flora and our fauna are world famous, ours alone –
And it's our job to look after them – some are already gone!

Family and home

The heart of lucky people's lives is family and home,
They might even be beside you as you read this silly poem.
All families are special, however big or small,
Some might be just your mum and you, others might fill a hall.

Mums and dads, sisters, brothers, uncles, aunts and cousins,
Grans and gramps, nans and pas, count them up in dozens,
Sometimes its double mums at home, sometimes double dads,
They all have one intention, to keep you well and glad,
To keep you safe and care for you, to tuck you in at night,
To feed and clothe and love you – to hug and hold you tight.

A Place of Safety

Out there in the big world there's trouble and there's strife.
If you lived in some countries you'd be fearing for your life.
There are nations waging war, they don't seem to like each other –
It makes no sense, this fighting, brother against brother.

Some places have no rainfall, people live in desert land.
They long for crops and water, nobody can eat sand.
But we're a lucky country, it gives us what we need.
So what's the sense of fighting, there is no need for greed.

We have our laws, but only for those people who do wrong.
Elsewhere they might just lock you up for singing the wrong song.
We are far enough away to hope the wars will stay away
As we enjoy our place of peace, living from day to day.

Take Time off

There's nowhere better to have fun than in our golden land.
For one thing it's an island, so it's girt by sea and sand.
Our beaches are world famous, for swimming, surfing too,
For paddling, fishing, sailing – there's lots of things to do.

Then all around, in bush and towns, there are heaps of sports to play,
Like cricket, football, soccer, netball – enough to play all day!
Whatever sport you fancy, your local teams are there
To join you up so you can play, have fun and run and share.

Then there's books down at the library just waiting to be read.
It's homework first, then happy reading until you go to bed.
We love to hike and camp in bushland, with nature all around,
Out among the birds and bees, fresh air and peaceful sounds.

And if by chance you find that there is nothing left to do,
Well, look around and you will find it surely isn't true.

For Art's Sake

What is that up on the wall? A handsome piece of art.
Well, if you want to learn to paint you have to make a start.
All round the town there's groups who are enjoying finer things.
They're painting, singing, cooking, reading, doing Highland Flings!

Even writing awful poems can bring you inner joy -
Some may like it, some may not – but if you do, enjoy!
There's not one soul in this fair land without an inner being.
Some are thinking, some are doing, some are merely seeing.

So look upon that work of art, listen to that song.
The finer things of life are free, a club where all belong.

Fair Go

If you see a bully who wants to start a fight,
Say, 'Stand back, mate, you surely know that fighting isn't right.
'You'll just be causing trouble if you try to land a blow,
'So go away – Australia is the land of the Fair Go!'

We like to see a contest – just look at all the sport –
But we don't like sneaks and bullies, people of that sort.
We don't like liars either, or cheaters, thieves or swearers,
Or Ratbags, braggers, smarties, layabouts or sneerers.

So if you see a bully hit a kid, say, 'Back off, Joe!
'Australians want to live in a land of the Fair Go.'

Government is Good

Someone's got to run the place, there's some that say they can.
It's true we can't just wander on; all nations need a plan.
You need parents and a teacher or else you would run wild.
Australia is the same, it's just a bigger problem child.

And so we have a local council working near to home.
They pick up all our rubbish, don't allow stray dogs to roam,
Organise school crossing guards, trim trees and cut the grass,
And keep the street lights on so all can safely pass.

The State government takes over for buses, trains and trams,
 Highways, roads and footpaths, stopping traffic jams,
Helping old and lonely people, running hospitals and schools,
Maintaining law and order with police to keep the rules.

The government of the Commonwealth is the national Top Dog,
Looking out from Canberra's summer heat and winter fog.
They make the big important rules, and give out standing orders,
Paying for our soldiers, protecting our long borders,
Making sure that all is done to keep us on the rails,
And knowing that we'll tip them out, if their Big Picture fails.

See the World

We are so low down on the planet that we have to fly for hours
To get to far-off countries from this far-off land of ours!
London, New York, Honolulu, new sights and sounds and faces
We mingle in the tourist world, coming from all over.
If you want to see the sights you have to be a rover!

Mum and Dad might take you if they have the time and space
They might be working hard, though, just staying in one place.
Your turn will come when you have worked to save the money,
But after that you'll hurry back to this land of milk and honey.

Keeping Busy

Guess what keeps the country going. It is a thing called work.
A fair day's work for a fair day's pay. It doesn't do to shirk.
Some get down and dirty, digging ditches, laying bricks,
Some teach naughty children, hoping the knowledge sticks
Some that learn go on to earn the biggest pile of dollars –
Doctors, lawyers, poets, painters, journalists and scholars.

The luckiest ones are those who love what they are doing,
Like driving taxis, cooking dinners, keeping coffee brewing.
We get paid at least enough to live and play and eat,
To pay our taxes and give ourselves some holidays and treats.

And if you cannot get a job, don't see yourself as shirking,
We're only saying life is good if you have a chance of working.

A Helping Hand

Just sitting there, you might think you never will need help,
But when you're a little older you might have to give a yelp!
The good thing in Australia is that people are respected
And those that are in trouble will never be neglected.

Grandma and Pops might get too old and tired to cope,
The local council has a plan to give them help and hope.
Nurses and workers, meals on wheels, someone to call and care.
You mightn't think about it now; one day you might be there.

The old and unemployed are given money to get by,
The sick and sad and lonely have welfare standing by.
And sometimes younger families find the money has run down,
There are agencies with food and clothes, right there in the town.

So don't despair, there's someone there, you mustn't feel a failure—
We're here to lift you up again, the people of Australia.

A Bounteous Land

We've got wheat fields big as Europe, and I've got a hunch
We can give to all the whole world bananas by the bunch.
The sunny north's bananaland, and there's pineapples galore,
The cooler south does apples, pears and plums and many more.
And those who like a bit of meat can always have a treat
With lamb and beef and chicken, as much as they can eat.

The world here is your oyster too, if you like some tasty fish.
There's flathead, salmon, coral trout and much more on your dish.
So we're not going hungry, but what is there to wear?
Well, we've got wool and we've got cotton, so much that we can share.

And share we do, we load our ships with goods for overseas
And don't forget our dairy food – butter, milk and cream and cheese.
And then there is the heavy stuff - iron, silver, copper, gold.
We are a land of milk and honey, and riches yet untold.

Tolerance

In our country there are different people round the town
From many lands and colours of black and white and brown.
Some have been here from the start, first people of the nation,
Others came to colonise, and more by immigration.

Many languages are now mingled as people learn and live
With different skills and customs, with great cuisine to give
Of pasta, pho, souvlaki, wiener schnitzel and chow mein,
Sushi and sashimi, bush tucker and terrine.

All wonderful surprises from all corners of the globe
They have enriched our culture, now we're far less xenophobic.

The Spirit

We are not just flesh and blood you know, there's something else in there.
You cannot see or touch it, but you know it's there somewhere.
It's something called the spirit, the soul or inner self.

It's born and lives within us, it's better far than wealth,
It guides our feelings and our actions, our desire to do what's right.
Whatever your religion, at our core we are just one.
We are all of nature's children in our playground of the sun.

A Faraway Land

We are the land that's far away, the place they call down under.
The explorers only found us when the sailors made a blunder,
Sailed downwards to this funny land, hopped out to look around,
Saw bits of desert, rocks and trees, then guess just what they found.

People, looking worried that they might have come to stay,
Saying to each other – we wish they'd go away.
But come they did, and brought their funny customs and controls
They drove the old ones off their land with bullets and patrols.

Those first people are still here, their culture still alive.
It's time to celebrate them, help them grow again and thrive,
For we have wealth and distance, let everyone decide
We are the new Australians, together in our pride.

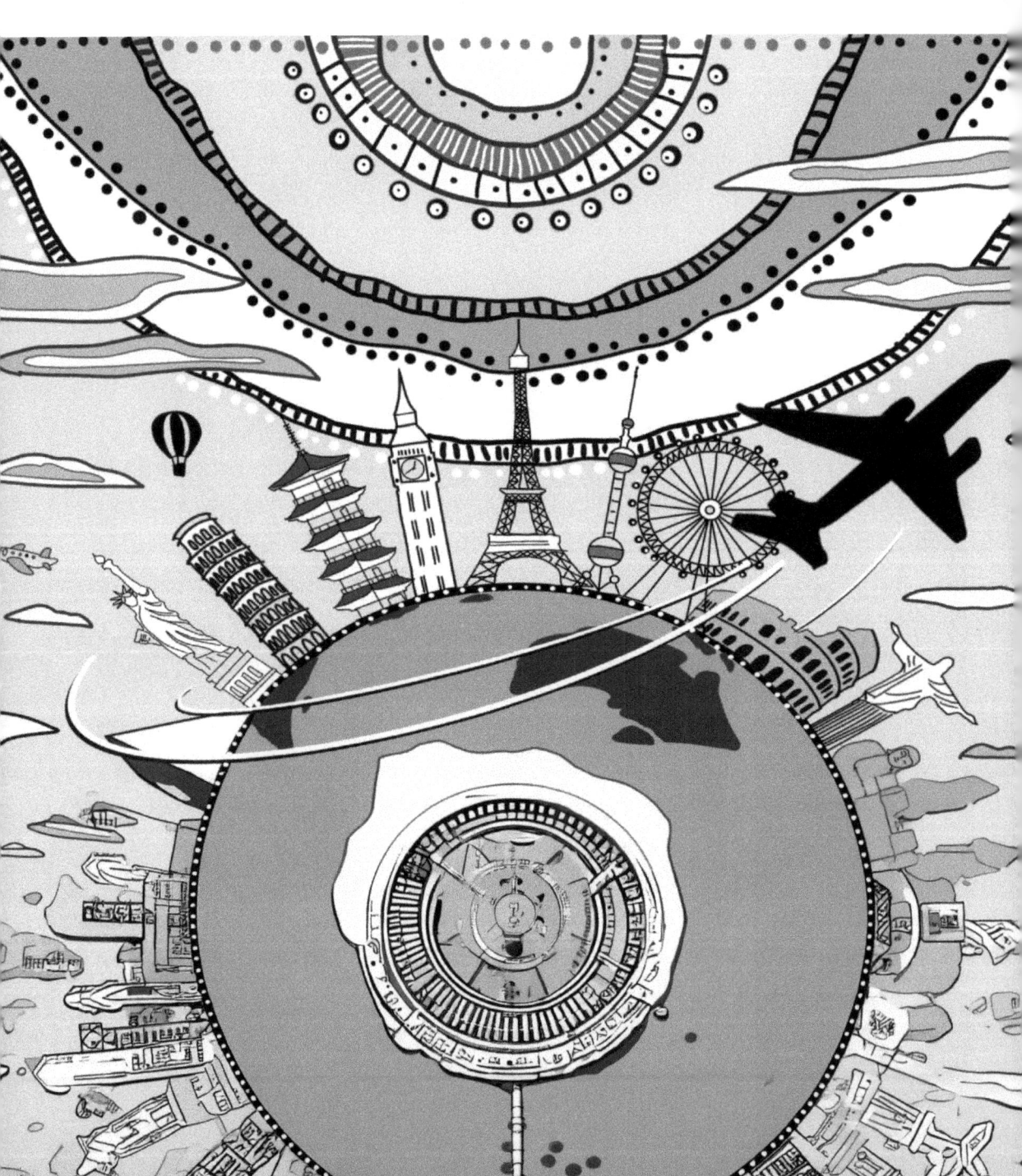

Moving On

Not many things are standing still – maybe a house, maybe a bush.
Most things are flying along a path, the world seems in a rush.
Trams and trains are on their tracks, aeroplanes are in the air,
Destination near or far, they are all hurrying somewhere.

And life's like that that for all of us, every second on the move.
Every breath and every thought, we are in our special groove.
Up in the morning, out in the day, working, playing, thinking,
Breakfast, lunch and dinner too, munching, crunching, drinking.

Life's not a race, it's a steady pace and we hope to keep control
With making calls on vital things, the things that make us whole:
Friendships, family, study, work – getting jobs done right away,
Having fun, having a laugh and dancing the night away.
And so it is, the time has come to give you all a break.
I've had my time, so you can say, 'Move on, for heaven's sake!!

John Ross is a former journalist, magazine editor, book publisher and writer. His 21 books include *Voices of the Bush*, *The Sounds of Melbourne* and *Every Picture tells a Story*. He was Editor in Chief of *Chronicle of the 20th Century* and *100 Years of AFL Football*.

Lucky Country
Author: John Ross

Text copyright © 2025 John Ross
Illustrations © 2025 Darya Kazakova

The moral rights of the creators have been asserted. All rights reserved. This publication (or any part of it) may not be reproduced or transmitted, copied, stored, distributed or otherwise made available by any person or entity in any form (electronic, digital, optical, mechanical) or by any means (photocopying, recording, scanning, or otherwise) without the written permission of the publisher.

ISBN:
978-1-922872-56-2 (print)

Wellington (Aust) Pty Ltd
ABN 30 062 365 413
433 Wellington Street
Clifton Hill, Victoria 3068
AUSTRALIA
www.kidzbookhub.com

www.ingramcontent.com/pod-product-compliance
Lightning Source LLC
Chambersburg PA
CBHW061147070526
44584CB00033B/4448